FASHION VICTIM STREET

Coloring Book

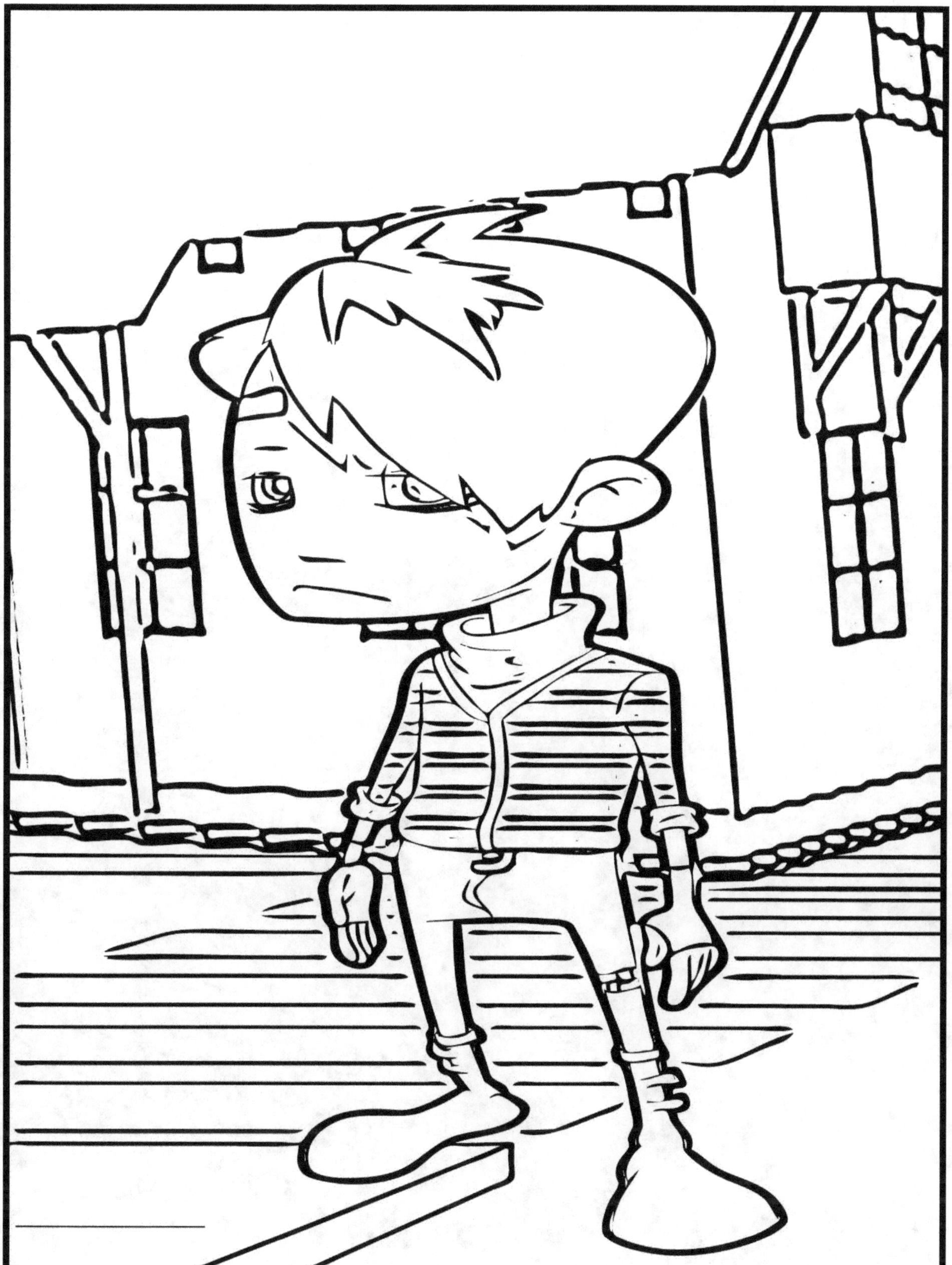

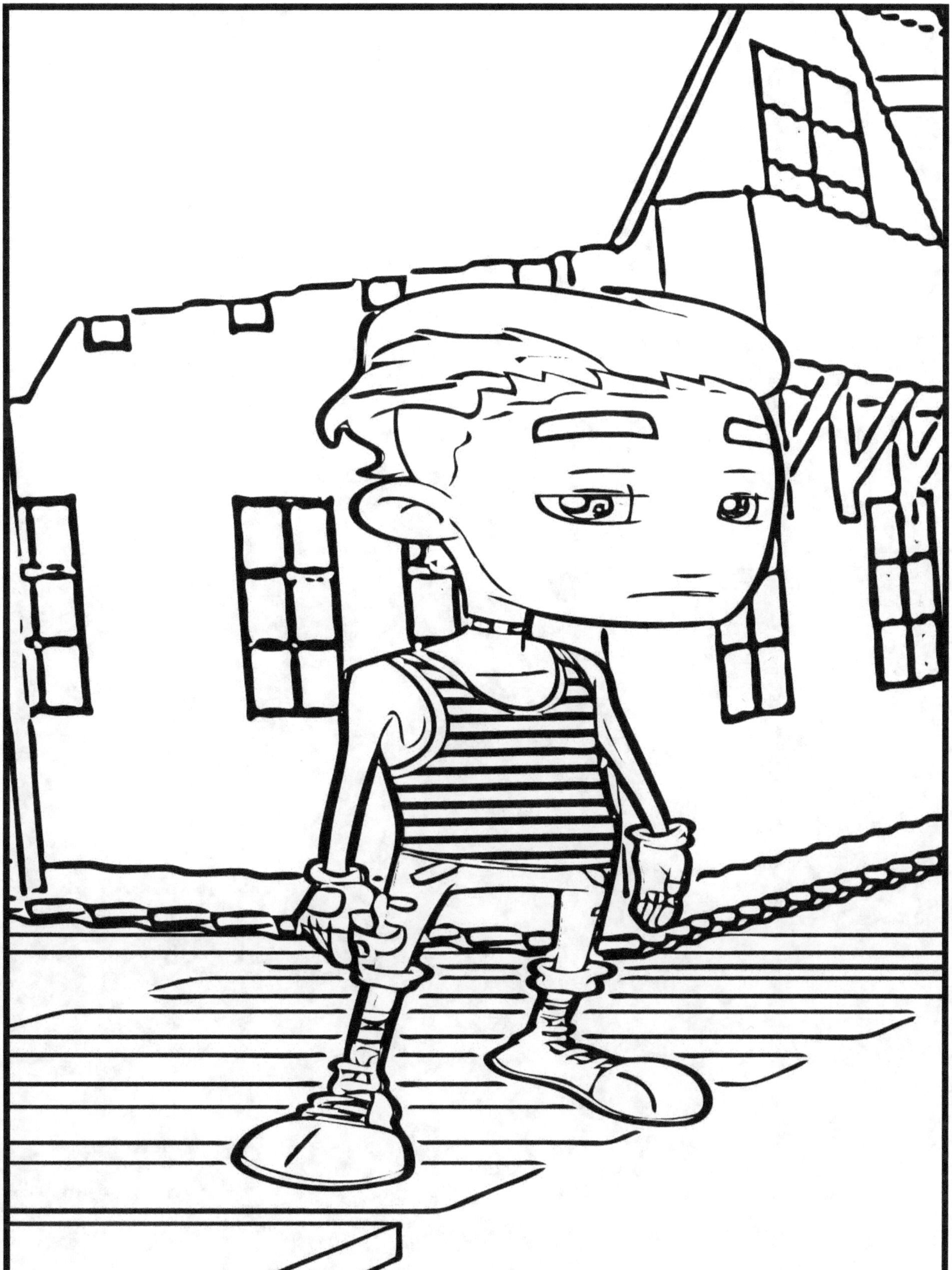

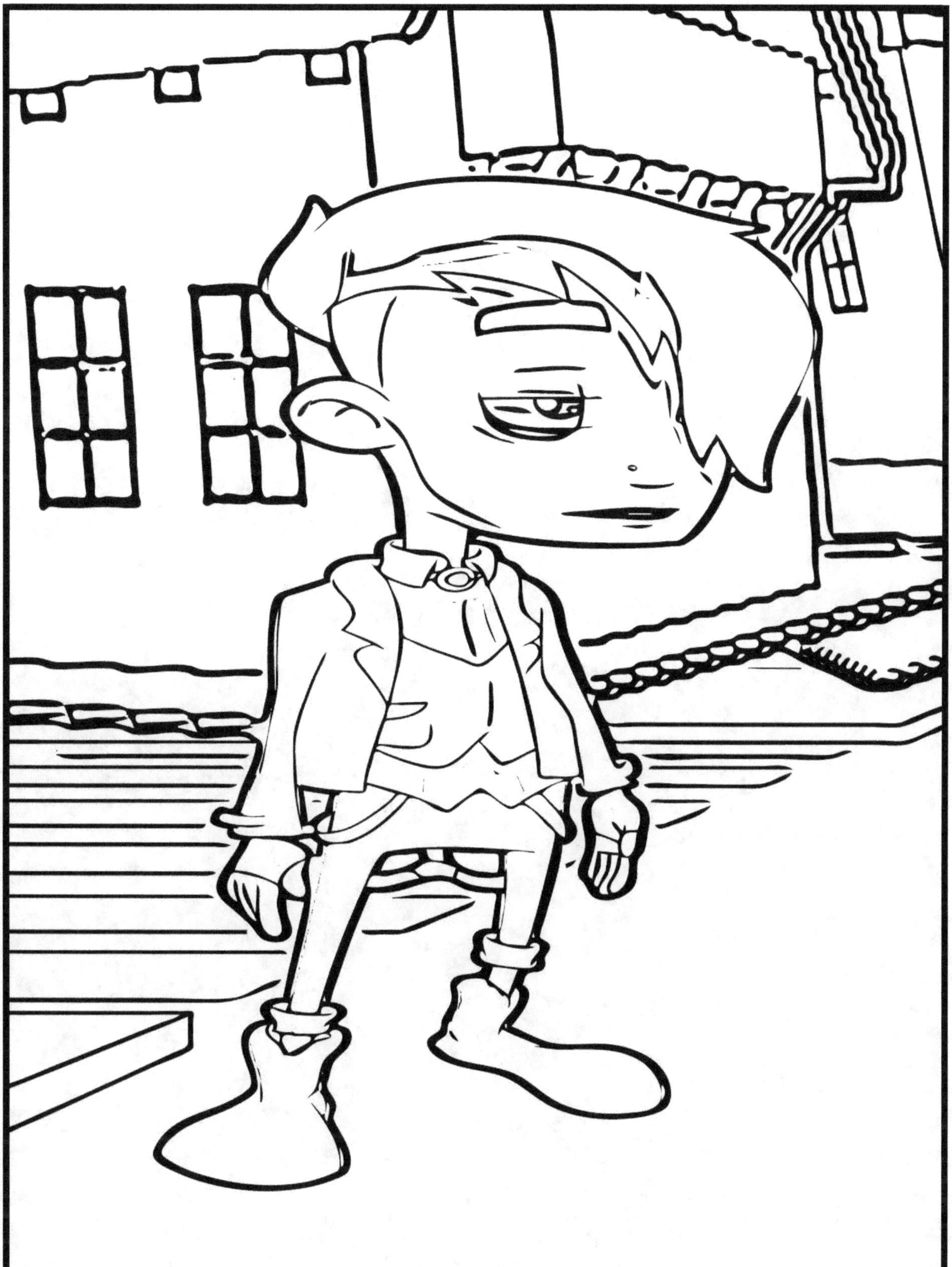

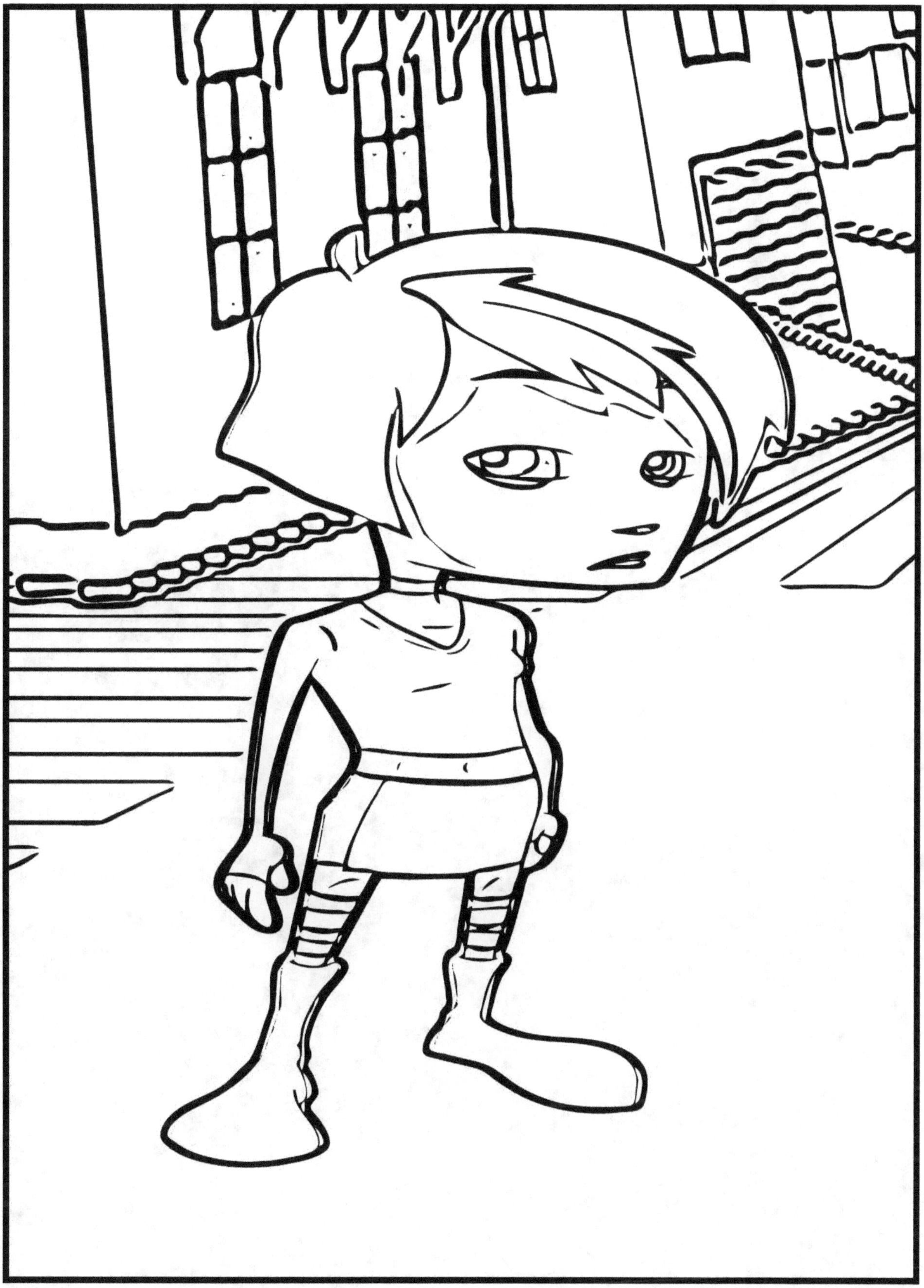

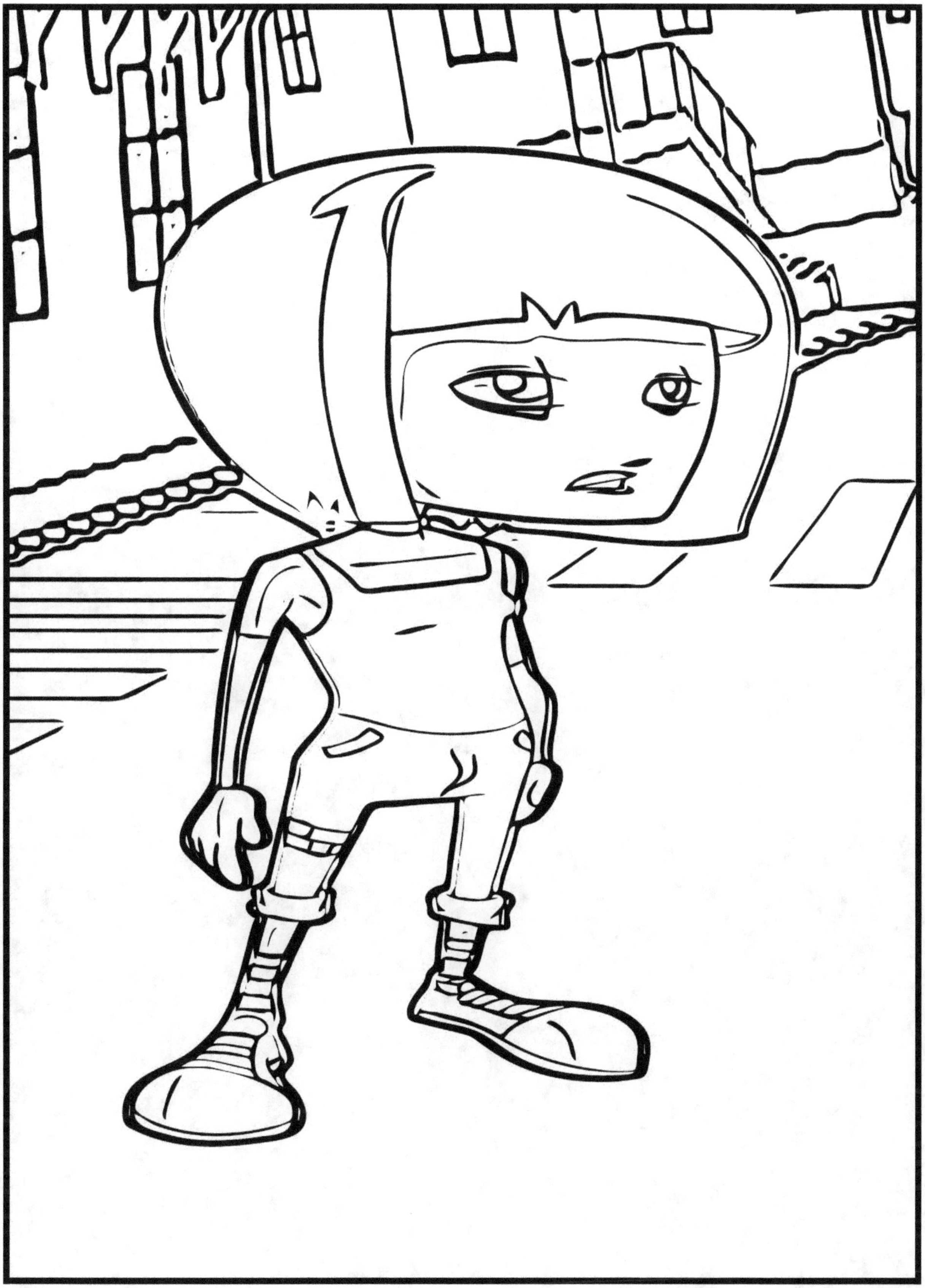

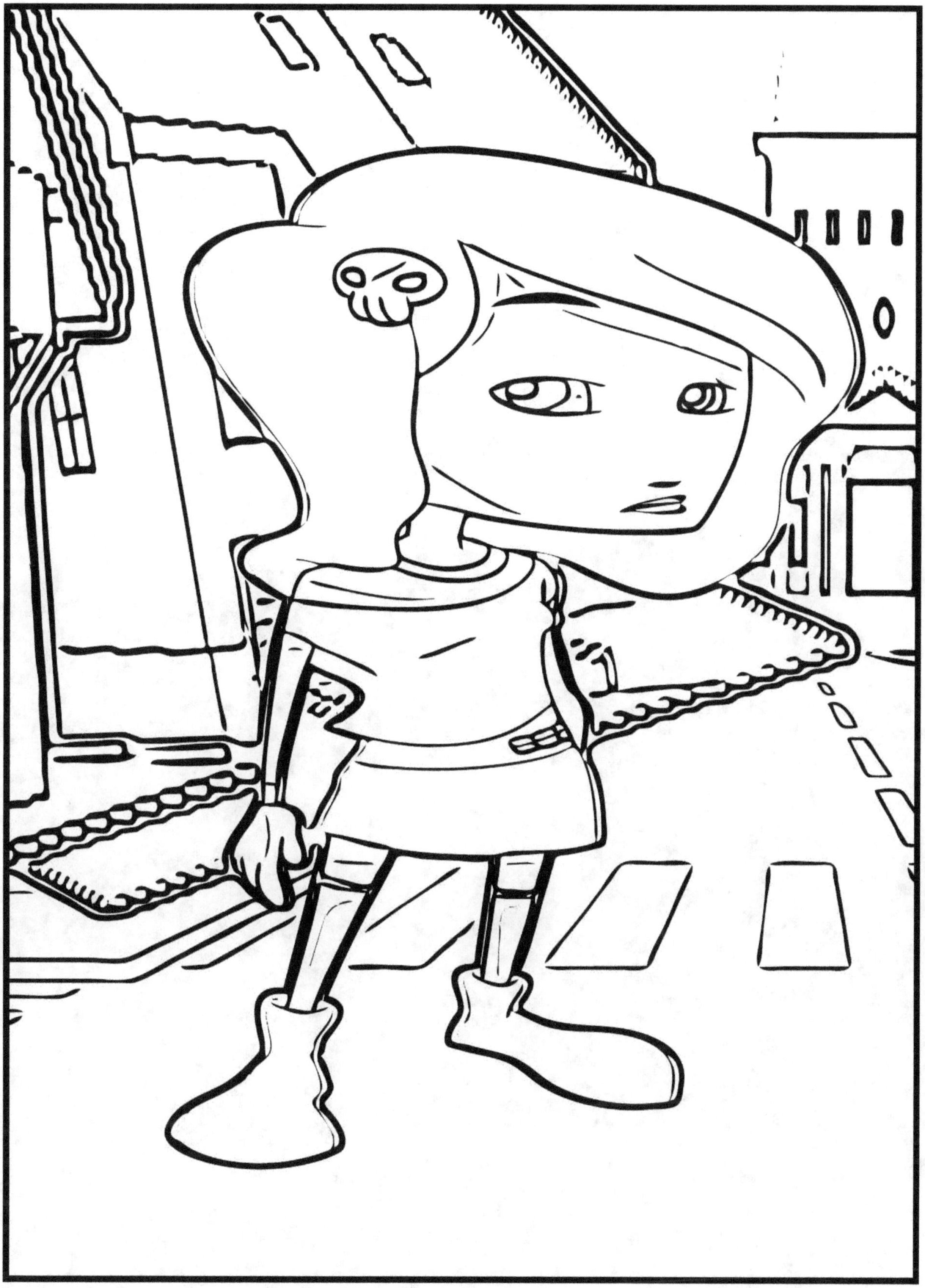

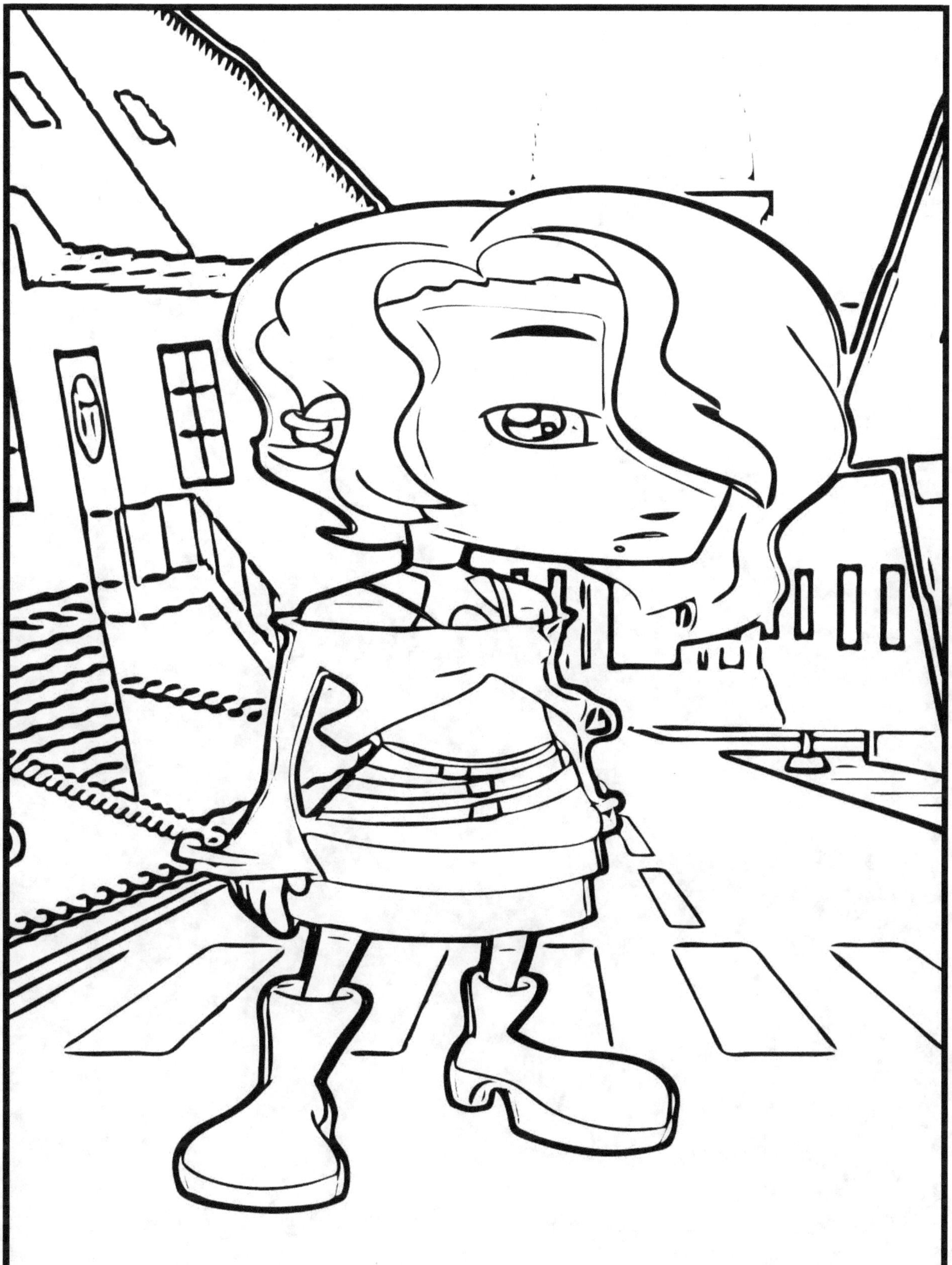

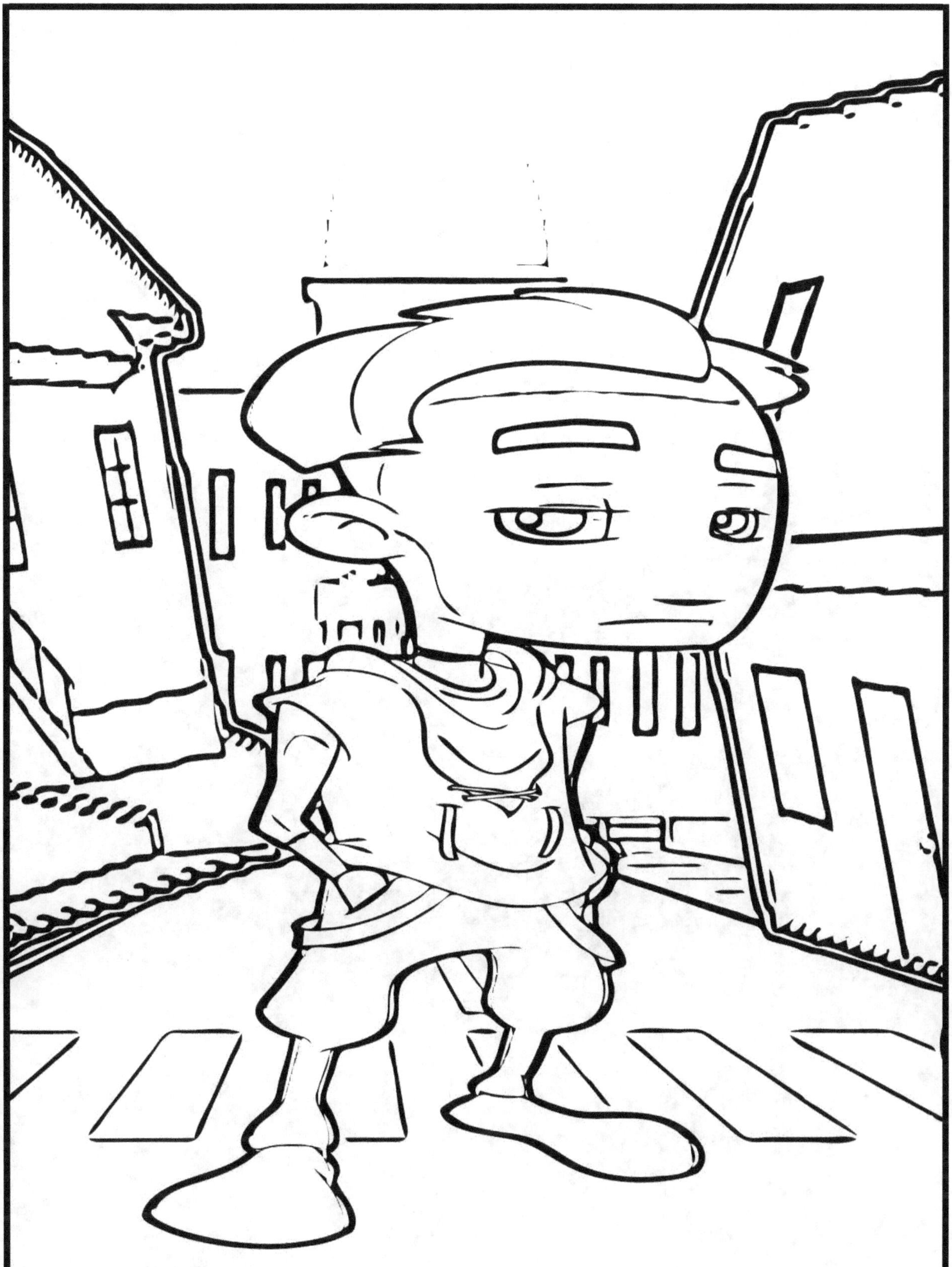

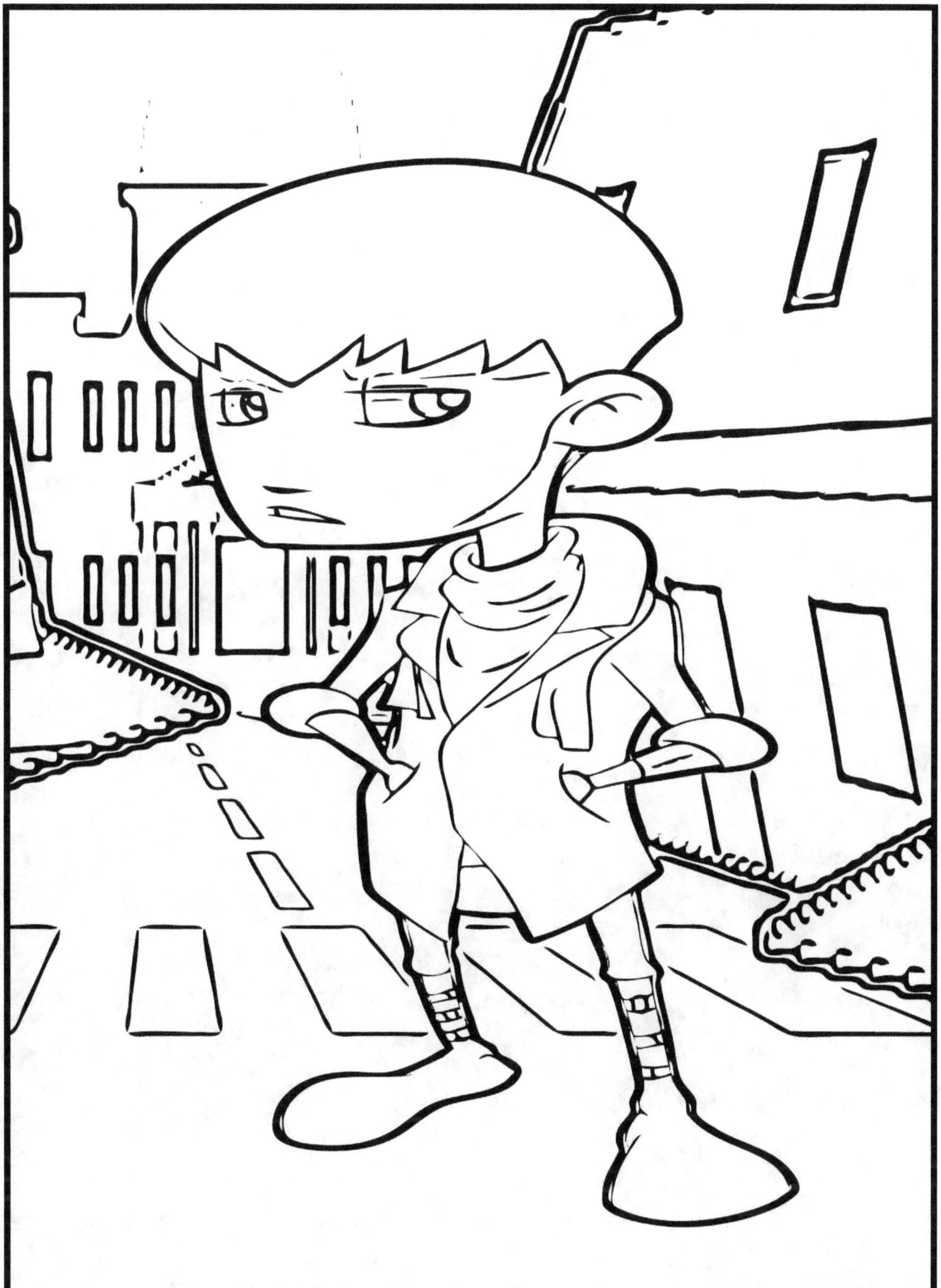

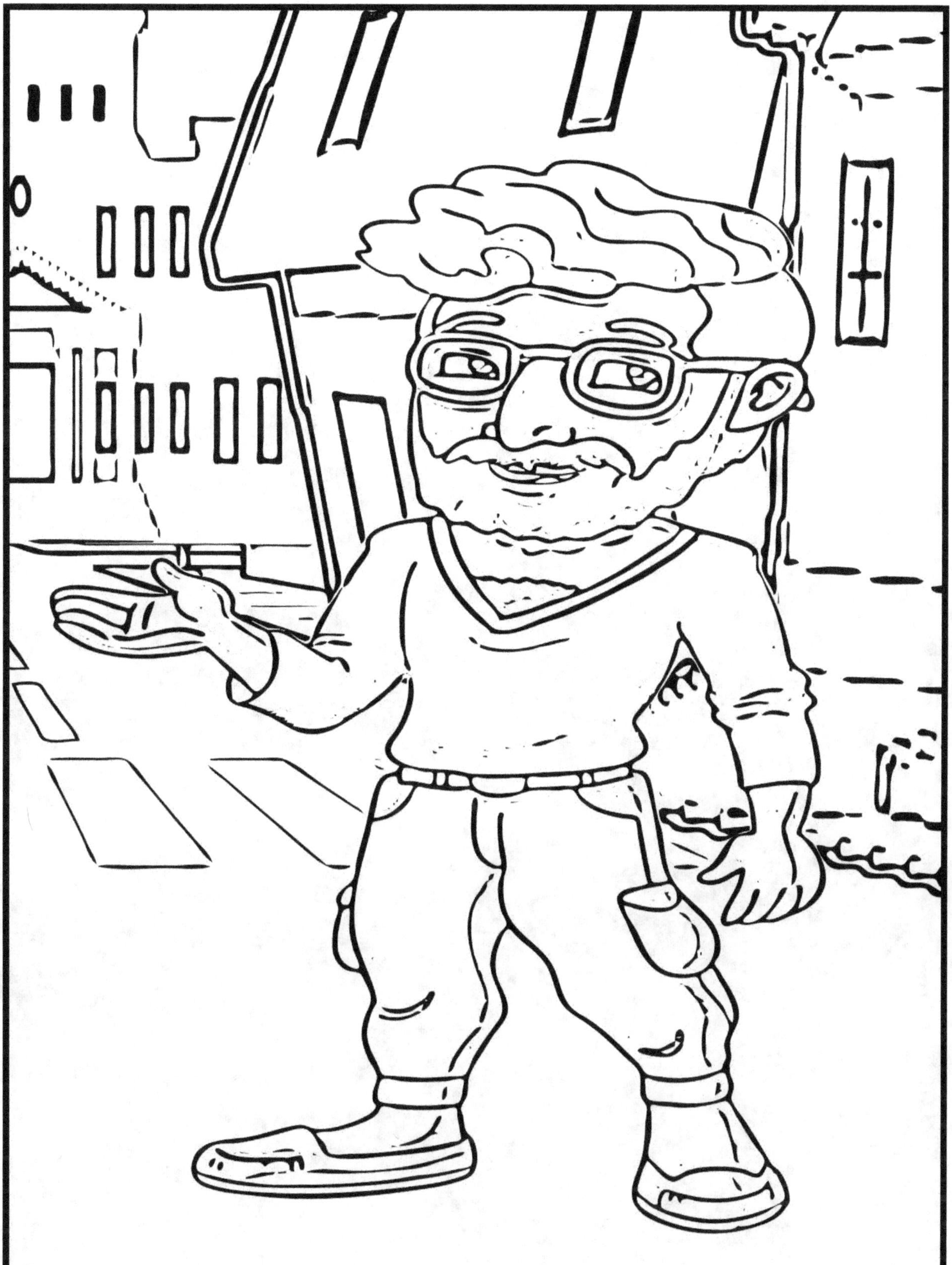

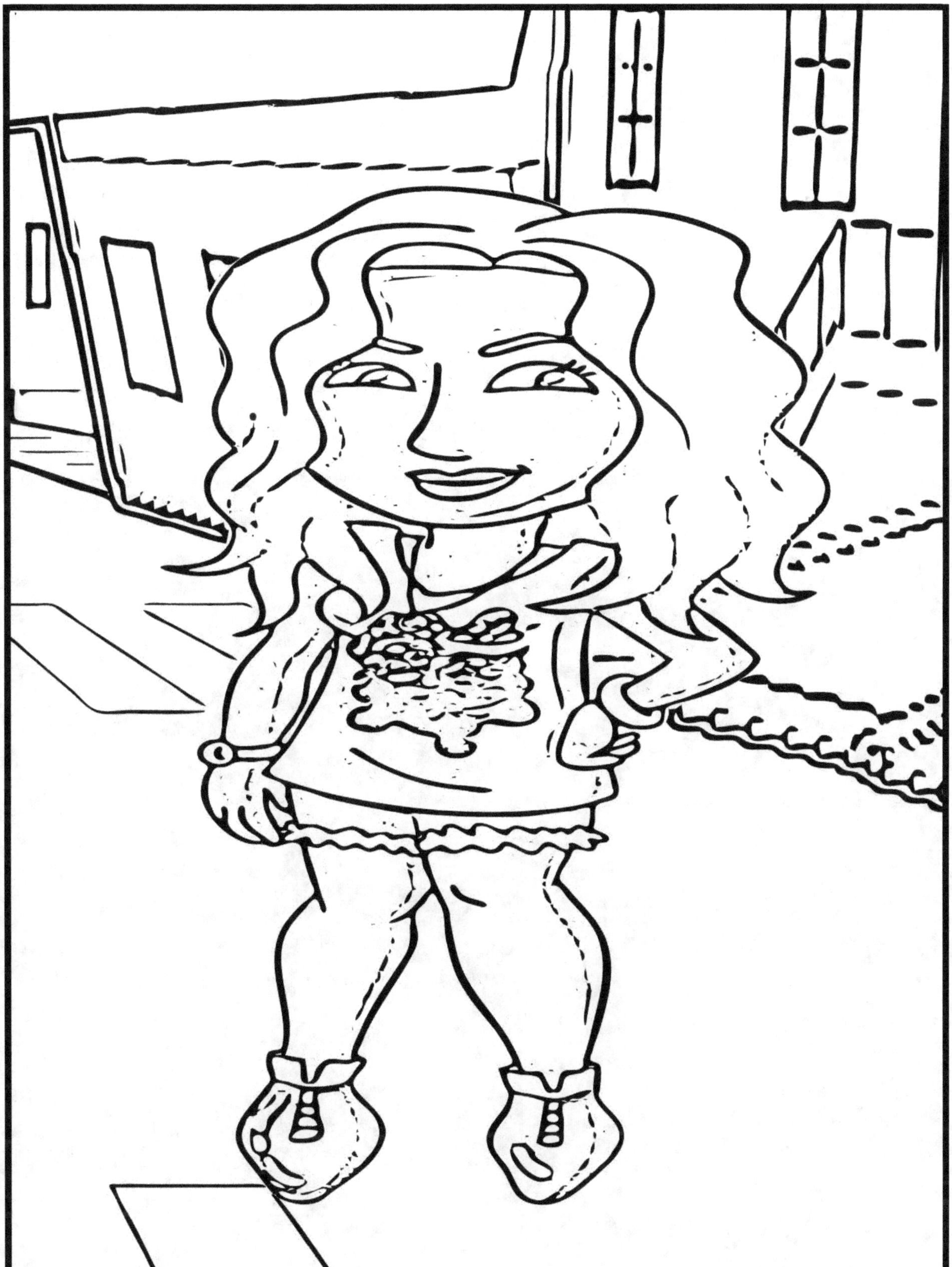

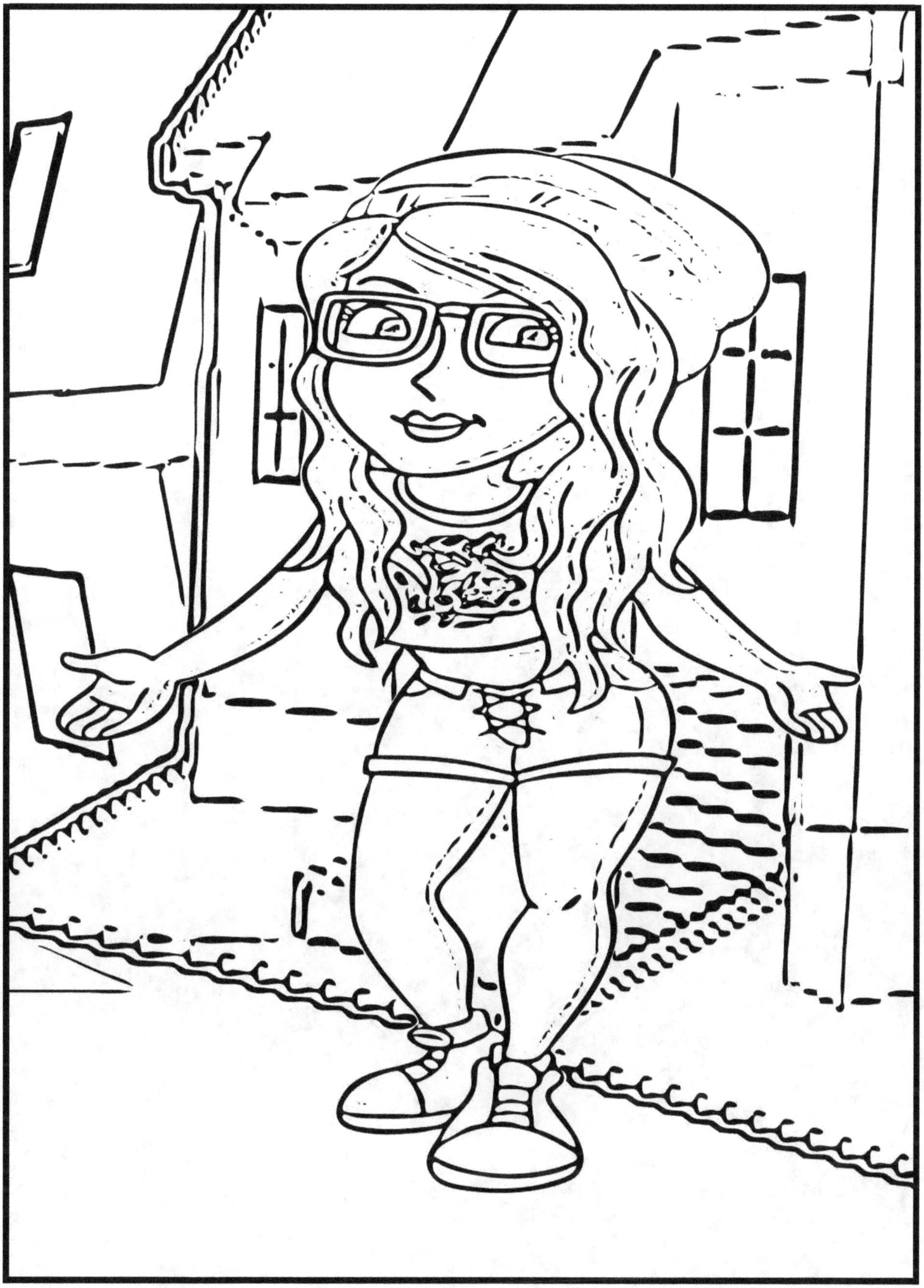

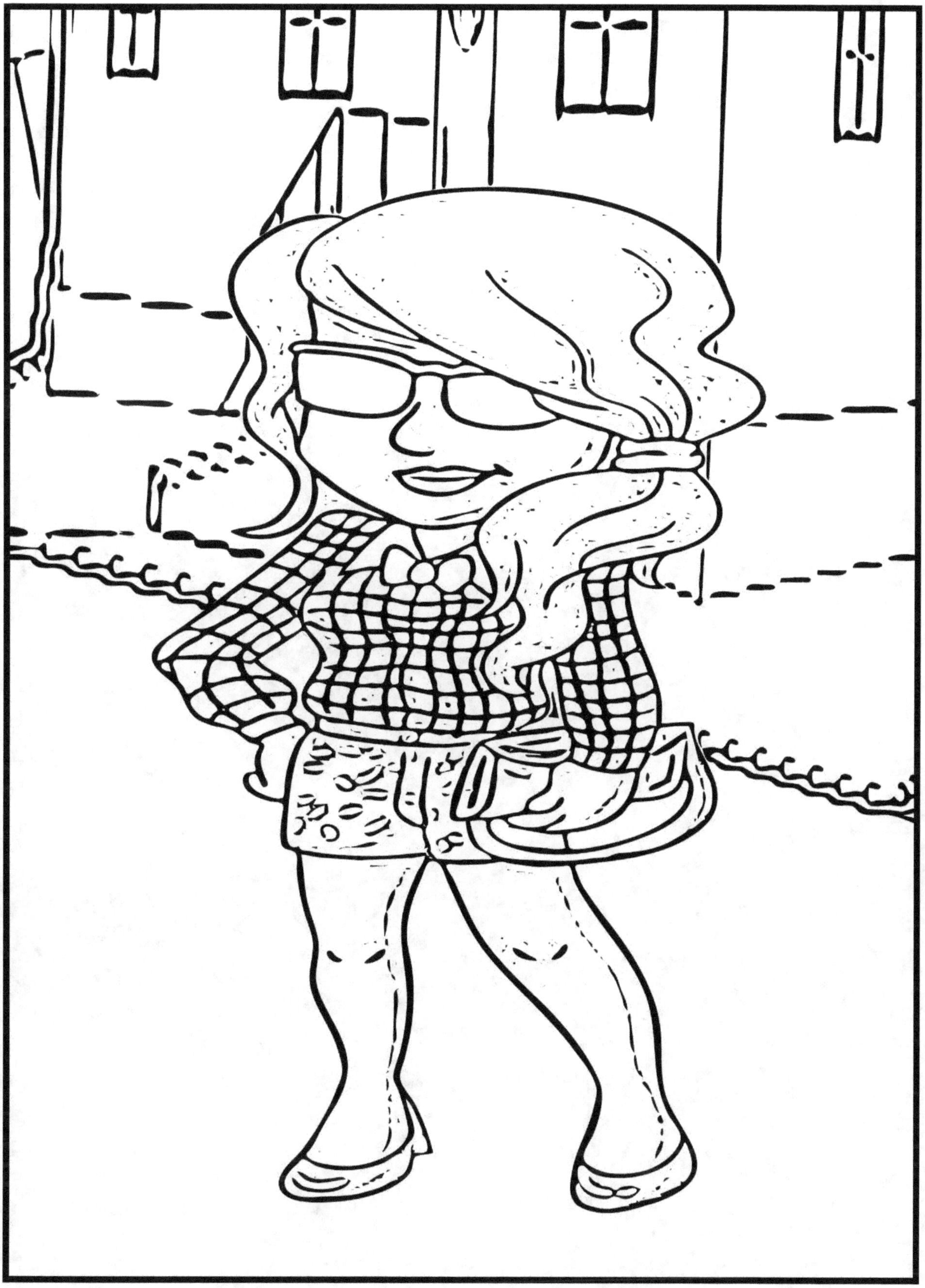

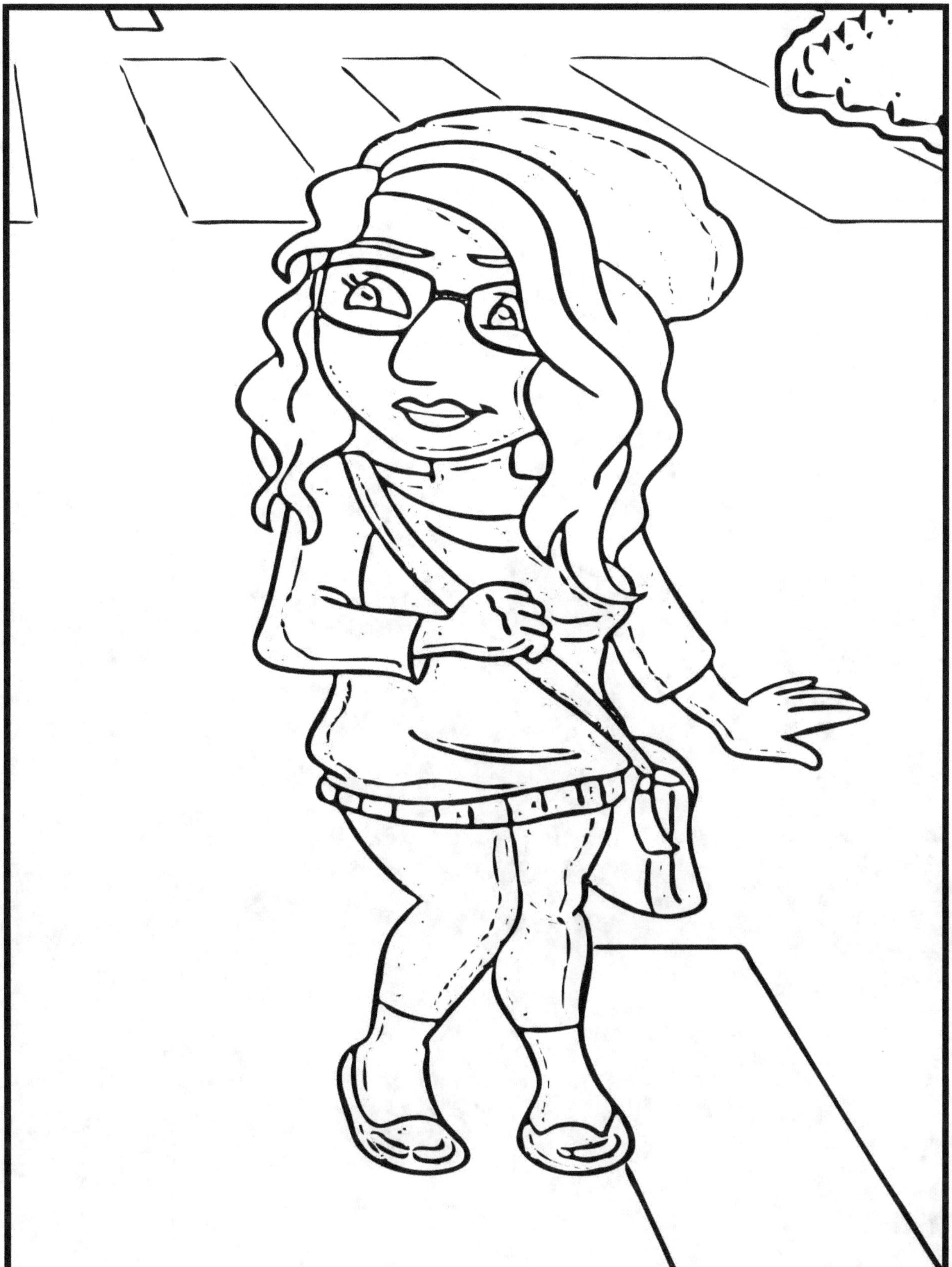

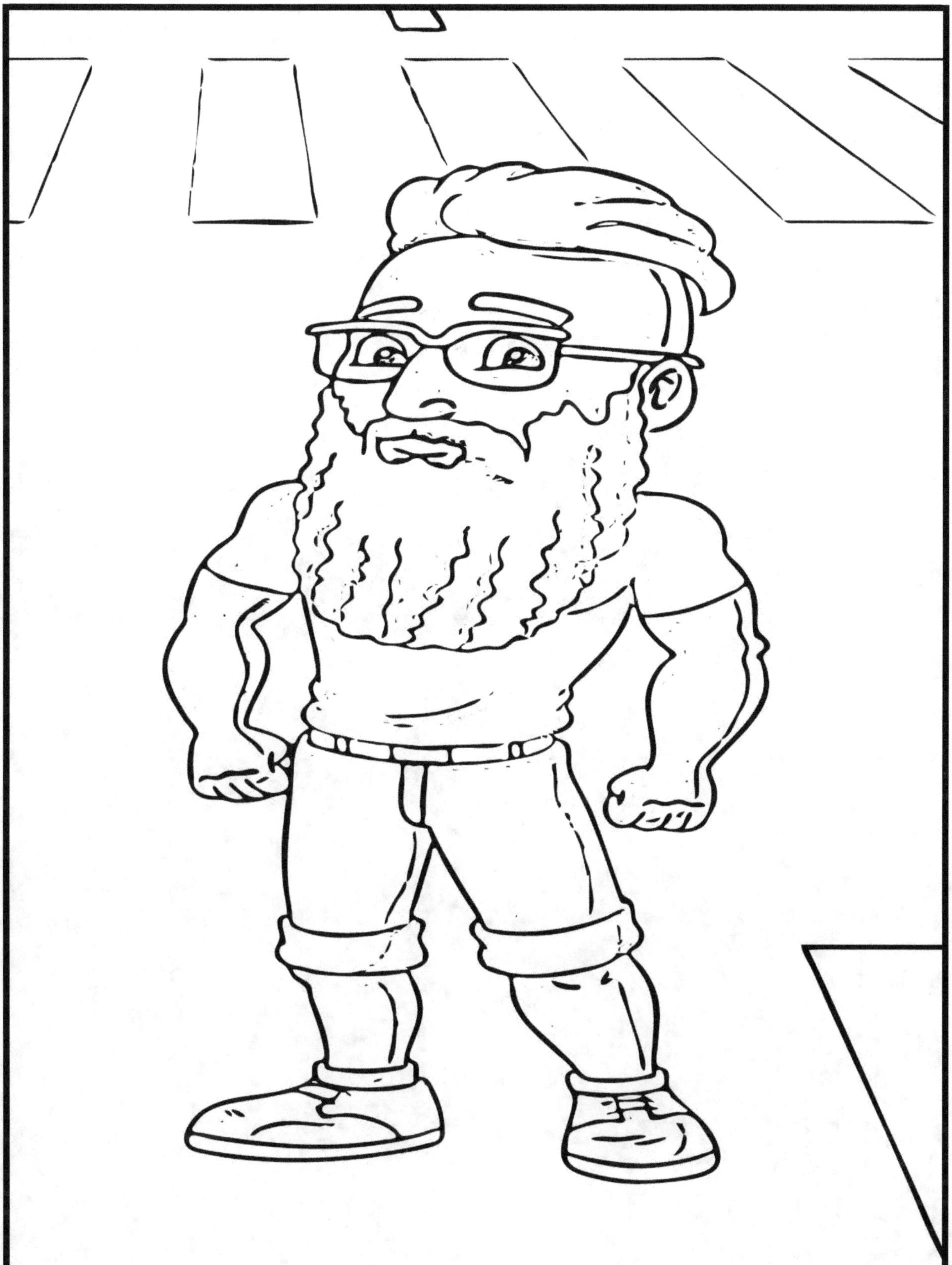

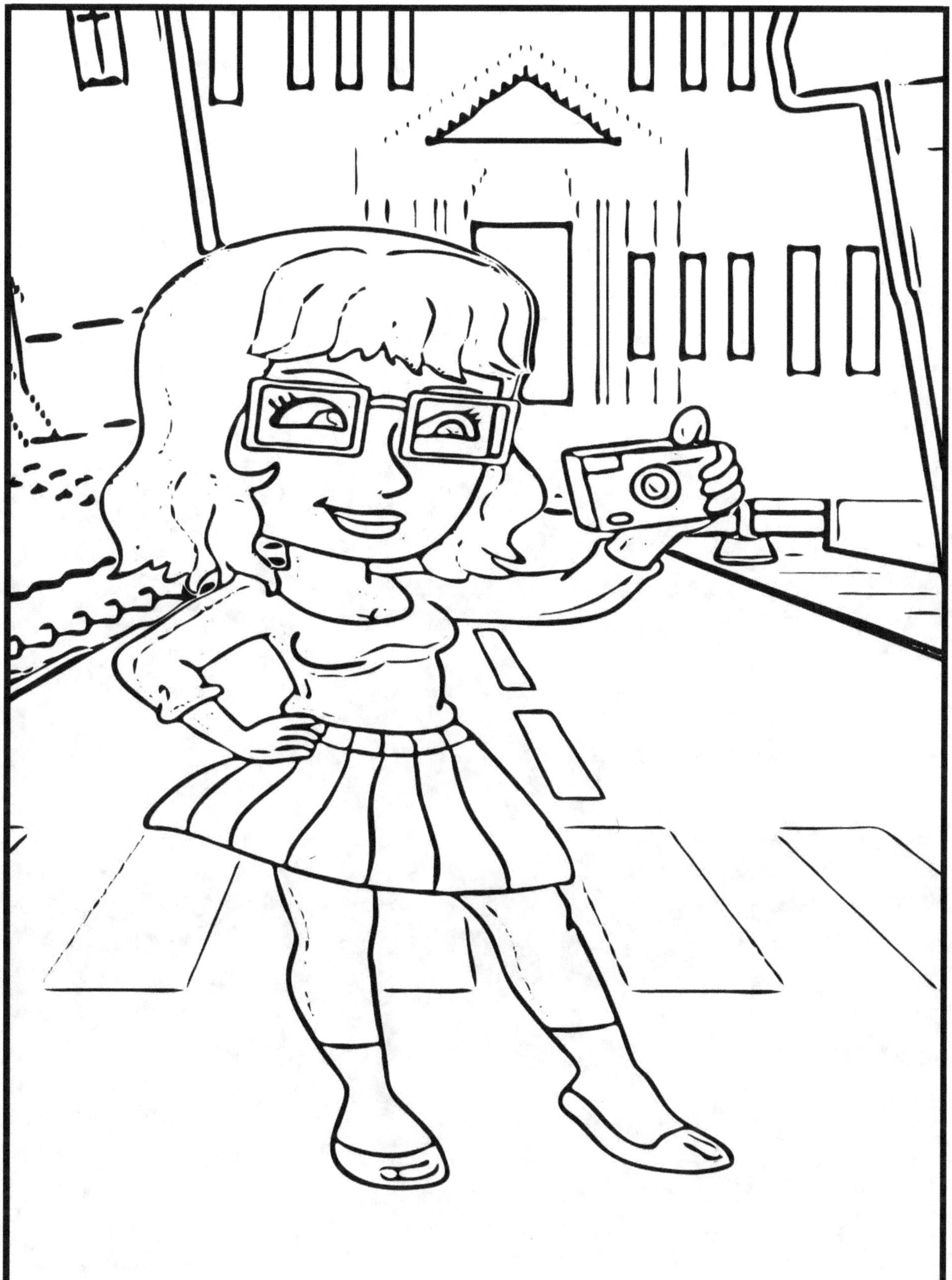

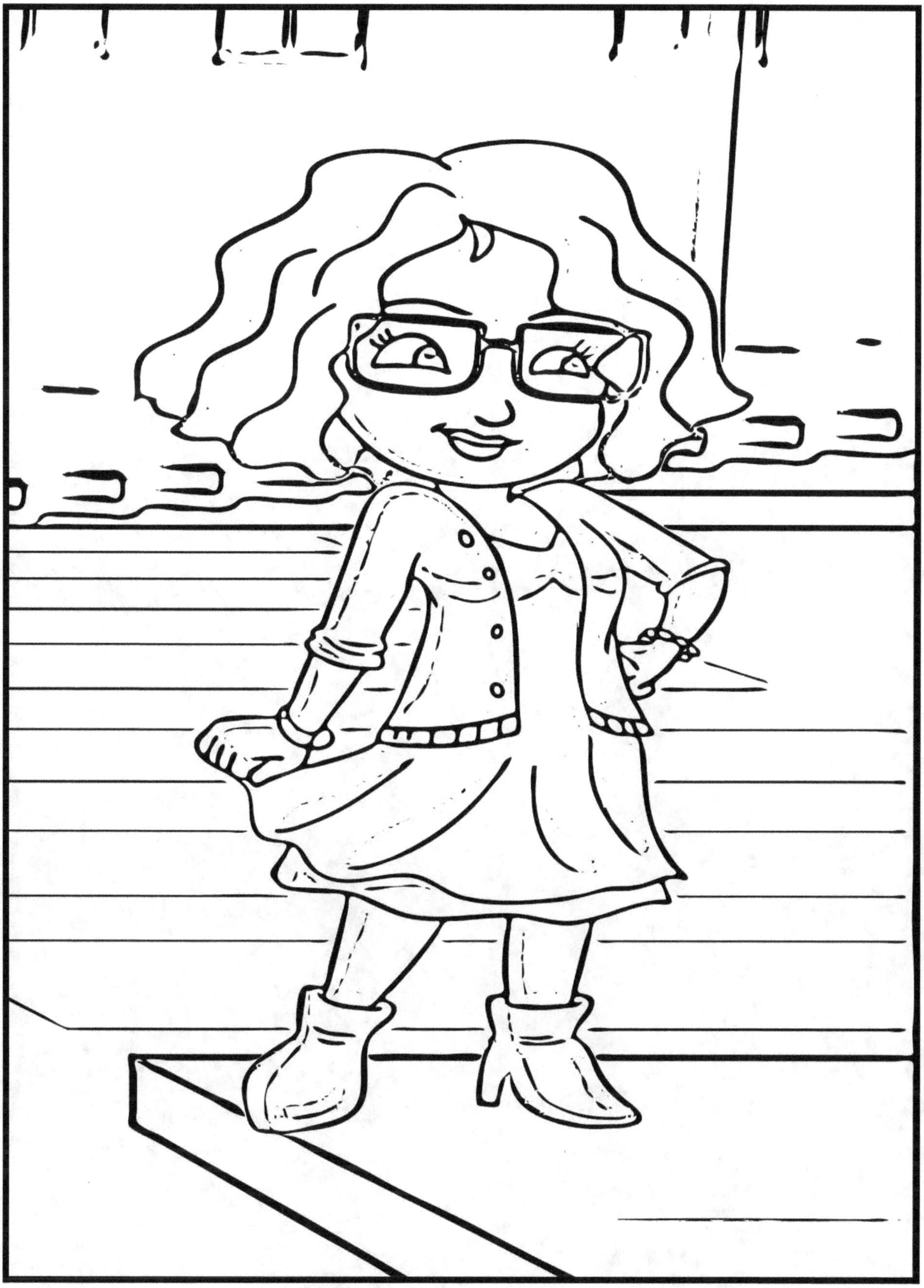

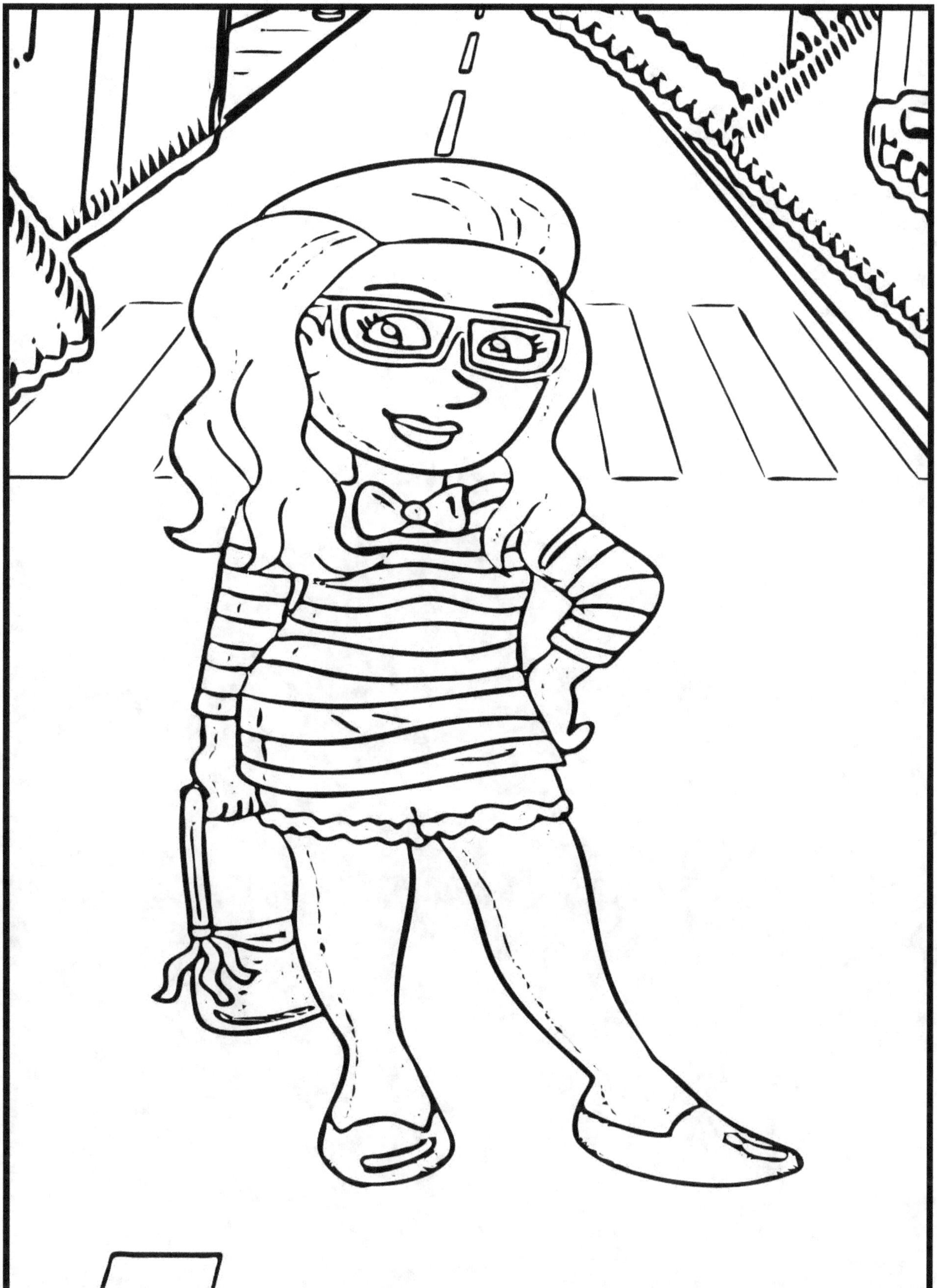

www.ingramcontent.com/pod-product-compliance
Lightning Source LLC
Chambersburg PA
CBHW081406170526
45166CB00010B/3229
* 9 7 8 1 5 1 9 3 3 1 7 2 4 *